What Took You So Long?

WHAT TOOK YOU SO LONG?

AN ASSORTMENT OF LIFE'S EVERYDAY IRONIES

WORDS BY *Sheldon Kopp*   PHOTOGRAPHS BY *Claire Flanders*

SCIENCE AND BEHAVIOR BOOKS, INC. *Palo Alto, California*

Design: Anita Walker Scott

Original photographic printing: Claire Flanders

Type composition: Mercury Typography, Inc.

SCIENCE & BEHAVIOR BOOKS, Inc.
701 Welch Road, Palo Alto, Ca. 94306

International Standard Book Number: 0-8314-0056-0

Library of Congress Catalog Card Number: 79-63270

Introduction

WE ARE ALL TEMPTED to try to understand the seemingly senseless suffering that life provides for each of us. People have always searched for ways to overcome their helplessness. Long before Buddha was enlightened or Christ crucified and resurrected, ordinary men and women already struggled to free themselves from this wheel of sorrows, to reach a place beyond this vale of tears.

In India, old, old stories still are told of a Hindu holy man named Nārada who devoted his life to attaining the spiritual liberation of *Nirvāṇa*. Tied to the slowly turning wheel of *Saṁsāra*, he had been trapped too long in the unending cycle of birth, life, death, and rebirth. He wanted only to free himself from attachment to *Māyā*, the illusion that is life, so that at last he might be released from the bondage of everyday existence.

In seeking *Nirvāṇa*, Nārada chose *Bhakti-Yoga* as his personal path. He had set himself a difficult task, but there is no easy way to attain *Nirvāṇa*. In order to find union with God, Nārada went to live simply and alone on a mountaintop where he could devote himself to uninterrupted meditation on the Divine Being. After years of austere and reverent concentration, the holy man had attained so high a level of spiritual liberation that he invited the fond attention of one of the three aspects of the Universal Lord.

And so it was that one day in that remote and barren hermitage, before the dedicated old man's eyes there appeared the object of his devotion, Vishṇu, the Preserver and Sustainer of the Universe. Delighted with Nārada's fulfillment of his many vows, Vishṇu said to him: "I have come to grant you a boon. Ask of me whatever you wish and it will be yours."

Joyfully, Nārada replied: "O Lord, if you are so pleased with me, there is one favor I would ask. I would like you to explain to me the secret of the power of *Māyā*, the illusion by which at the same time you both reveal and conceal the nature of the universe."

Vishṇu responded more gravely: "Good Nārada, other holy men before you have asked to be granted that same boon. Believe me, it never works out very well. What would you do with comprehension of my *Māyā* anyway? Why not ask for something else? You can have anything you like."

But Nārada insisted that nothing would do but that he should come to learn the power of *Māyā* so that he would forever after understand the secret of how attachment to illusion creates needless suffering.

"Very well, then," answered Vishṇu. "Have it your own way." An ambiguous smile played along his beautifully curved lips. "Come with me to the place where you will learn the power of *Māyā*."

Together they left the pleasant coolness of the sheltering hermitage roof, descended the steep wooded slope, and headed out beyond the valley. Under a mercilessly scorching sun, Vishṇu led Nārada across a barren stretch of desert. It was many hours before they came to a place of shade. Vishṇu stretched out on a cool spot on the sand, saying: "It is here that you will learn the power of *Māyā*."

Nārada was about to sit at the Lord's feet to be instructed when Vishṇu said: "I am so thirsty. Before we begin, I would like you to take this cup and go fetch me some cool water."

Always ready to serve his master, Nārada took the empty cup and went off over a rise in search of water. Just beyond that dune, unexpectedly the holy man came upon a fertile valley. At the near edge of the abundantly cultivated fields was a small tree-shaded cottage. Beside it was a well. Delighted at his good fortune, Nārada knocked at the cottage door to ask permission to fill his cup from the well.

But the door was opened by a maiden so beautiful that the old man immediately became enthralled. Lost in the enchantment of her eyes, he stood there too dazed to remember why he had come to the cottage in the first place.

But no matter. She seemed as taken with him as he with her. Inviting him to enter with a voice so compelling that he could not refuse, the maiden made him welcome. Introducing him to the rest of her family, she insisted that he stay for dinner. Though he had just arrived as a stranger, Nārada soon felt as if he were at home among good and trusted friends. Easily transformed from unbidden visitor to house-guest, he stayed on as one comfortable day followed the next. Inevitably, the holy man and the maiden fell in love and after a time they married.

Twelve years passed. When his wife's father died, Nārada took over the farm. The crops were more abundant each season, and during those years three beautiful children were born to this loving couple. Nārada had everything that anyone might want. This was the happiest time of his entire life.

The twelfth year turned out to be a time of natural disasters. An extraordinarily violent rainy season resulted in flooding that destroyed the crops and swept away the thatched huts. One night the farm-hands fled. The next morning the torrents rose until even the high ground of Nārada's own cottage had to be abandoned.

Their youngest child perched on his shoulder, one hand supporting his wife while with the other he led his two older children, Nārada waded out into the swirling thigh-high waters. Losing his footing in the slippery mud, he lurched forward, pitching the smallest child from his shoulder headlong into the swelling stream. In a desperate grab to try to save the baby, Nārada released his hold on his wife and their other children. The baby was swept away in the rushing waters, and the others along with him.

None could be saved. All were gone. How could it be? Nārada had been the happiest of men. He had had a lovely wife and three wonderful children. Now all were drowned. He had become the most successful farmer in the whole valley, and now the crops were gone as were his friends and his home.

Weeping in bewilderment and feeling more sorrow than he had experienced in all of his life, Nārada stood dazedly midst the waters swirling up above his knees. Alone and devastated, he knew that everything and everyone he cared about were lost to him forever.

And then all at once the swirling currents were gone. Looking down at the dry sand beneath his feet, Nārada saw that the only water that remained filled a small cup that unaccountably appeared in his hand. He was startled to hear a familiar voice. Looking up, just ahead of him he saw Vishṇu stretched out in a shady spot on this barren desert. Smiling serenely, Vishṇu asked teasingly: "Sweet Nārada, what took you so long?"

What Took You So Long?

Often things *are* as
bad as they seem.

Even so, some of the time
it's possible to enjoy life as it is.

But the better anything gets, the more you'll miss it when it's gone.

Why grieve, when nothing helps? We cry *because* nothing helps.

If you stubbornly refuse to mourn your losses, you get depressed.

Revenge is a form of nostalgia.

Suicide can be a case of mistaken identity

What's a person to do about
feeling helpless? For a while
there's just no way to see
what's funny about being stuck.

At last you cry out in anguish:
"Why me?" God answers: "Why not?"

You can *so* stand it.

After all, it's only pain.

What makes it seem unbearable
is your mistaken belief that it can be cured.

Everything is difficult at first.

I have never begun any important venture for which I felt adequately prepared.

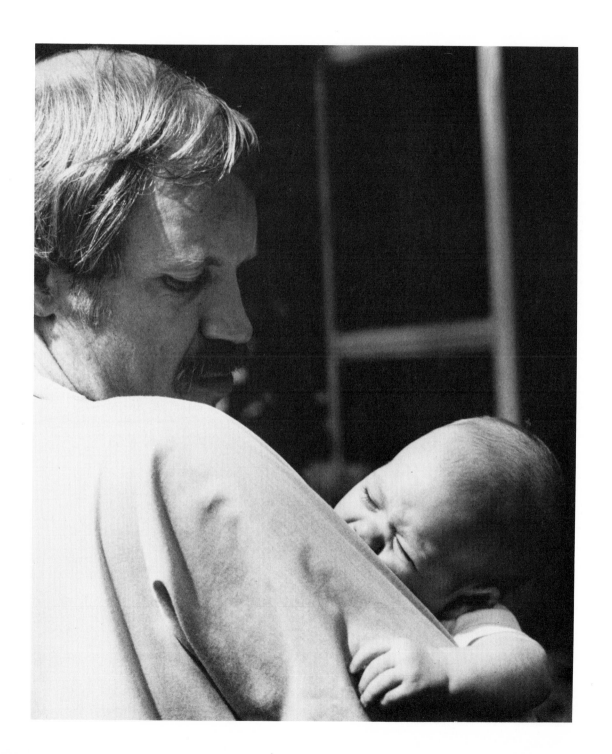

Not everything worth doing is worth doing well.

Without knowing for sure what's right or wrong,
take your best shot.

There's just no way to get it all straight. Mistakes are inevitable.

Control is an illusion.

You wait for everything to be all right,
knowing all the while
that the next problem is already in the mail.

Life just keeps coming at you.

Complaining can become a way of boasting
about how much suffering you can endure.

If we allow pain more
of our attention than it
requires, we miss
some opportunities for joy.

Escape is not a dirty word.
None of us can face what's happening
head-on all of the time.

It's all right to pretend sometimes. The only danger lies in pretending that you are not pretending.

There's nothing to figure out. Life is not *about* anything.

The answers keep changing.
The questions remain the same.

Straightforward words seem paradoxical.

We don't have to talk to pass the time.

The time will pass

in any case.

Remember, we are all in this alone.

It helps to know
that everyone is
in the same situation.
It helps,
but not a whole lot.

Unable to get our own way, often we settle for trying
to prevent other people from getting their way.

We insist that *our* situation is special. It's so hard to accept how ordinary we all are.

By now, I'm no longer interested in whether
or not someone *really* loves me.
I'll settle for being treated well.

I don't even mind
being manipulated, so long
as it feels good.

We must learn to love in the absence of illusions.

We must try to live a just life in an unjust world.

We must be willing
to go on caring even
when we are helpless
to change things.

Our best may not turn out to be good enough. Still it will have to do.

I'm not OK. You're not OK. And that's OK.

Biographical Notes

SHELDON KOPP is a psychotherapist and teacher of psychotherapy in Washington, D.C. He received his Ph.D. in Psychology from the New School for Social Research, and for twenty-four years has served as a guide for the troubled in prisons, hospitals, clinics, and in private practice. Dr. Kopp is also the author of *Guru: Metaphors from a Psychotherapist*, published in 1971; *If You Meet the Buddha on the Road, Kill Him*, published in 1972; *The Hanged Man: Psychotherapy and the Forces of Darkness*, published in 1974; *No Hidden Meanings*, also in collaboration with Claire Flanders, published in 1975; *This Side of Tragedy: Psychotherapy as Theater*, published in 1977; and *Back to One: A Practical Guide for Psychotherapists*, also published in 1977 by Science and Behavior Books.

CLAIRE FLANDERS was born and raised in France where she studied drama and music. Marriage to an American brought her to this country in 1956. She first became interested in photography as the record-keeper of her family. Now she is working full time as a freelance photographer. *No Hidden Meanings*, also in collaboration with Sheldon Kopp, was published in 1975 by Science and Behavior Books. Mrs. Flanders lives in Washington, D.C. with her husband; they have four children.

Posters, *No Nirvāṇa Without Samsāra* and *An Eschatological Laundry List*, of the texts of Sheldon Kopp's books, *What Took You So Long?* and *No Hidden Meanings*, can be ordered from: Yes! Bookshop, 1035 Thirty-first Street, Washington, D.C. 20007.